Rivers and Mountains   Jo

ALSO BY JOHN ASHBERY

Poetry

Some Trees
The Tennis Court Oath
Rivers and Mountains
The Double Dream of Spring
Three Poems
The Vermont Notebook
Self-Portrait in a Convex Mirror
Houseboat Days
As We Know
Shadow Train
A Wave
Selected Poems
April Galleons

Fiction

A Nest of Ninnies
(*with James Schuyler*)

Plays

Three Plays

Rivers and Mountains   John Ashbery

The Ecco Press   New York

This edition issued in 1977 by The Ecco Press
26 West 17th Street, New York, N.Y. 10011
Published simultaneously in Canada by
Penguin Books Canada Ltd., Ontario
Printed in the United States of America

Grateful acknowledgement is made to *Poetry* for permission
to reprint the following poems: *Civilization and Its Discontents,
A Blessing in Disguise, Last Month, The Recent Past, If the
Birds Knew*. Other poems were previously published in the
following periodicals: *Art and Literature, Location, Locus
Solus*, and *The Yale Literary Magazine*.

Cover drawing by Trevor Winkfield
Cover typography by Ronald Gordon

Library of Congress Cataloging in Publication Data
Ashbery, John.
   Rivers and mountains.
   (The American poetry series; v. 12)
   I. Title.
PS3501.S475R5   1977   811'.5'4   76-46176
ISBN 0-88001-190-4

Third printing, 1988

Rivers and Mountains

Contents

These Lacustrine Cities

These lacustrine cities grew out of loathing
Into something forgetful, although angry with history.
They are the product of an idea: that man is horrible,
    for instance,
Though this is only one example.

They emerged until a tower
Controlled the sky, and with artifice dipped back
Into the past for swans and tapering branches,
Burning, until all that hate was transformed into useless love.

Then you are left with an idea of yourself
And the feeling of ascending emptiness of the afternoon
Which must be charged to the embarrassment of others
Who fly by you like beacons.

The night is a sentinel.
Much of your time has been occupied by creative games
Until now, but we have all-inclusive plans for you.
We had thought, for instance, of sending you to the middle
    of the desert,

To a violent sea, or of having the closeness of the others be air
To you, pressing you back into a startled dream
As sea-breezes greet a child's face.
But the past is already here, and you are nursing some private project.

The worst is not over, yet I know
You will be happy here. Because of the logic
Of your situation, which is something no climate can outsmart.
Tender and insouciant by turns, you see

You have built a mountain of something,
Thoughtfully pouring all your energy into this single monument,
Whose wind is desire starching a petal,
Whose disappointment broke into a rainbow of tears.

On the secret map the assassins
Cloistered, the Moon River was marked
Near the eighteen peaks and the city
Of humiliation and defeat—wan ending
Of the trail among dry, papery leaves
Gray-brown quills like thoughts
In the melodious but vast mass of today's
Writing through fields and swamps
Marked, on the map, with little bunches of weeds.
Certainly squirrels lived in the woods
But devastation and dull sleep still
Hung over the land, quelled
The rioters turned out of sleep in the peace of prisons
Singing on marble factory walls
Deaf consolation of minor tunes that pack
The air with heavy invisible rods
Pent in some sand valley from
Which only quiet walking ever instructs.
The bird flew over and
Sat—there was nothing else to do.
Do not mistake its silence for pride or strength
Or the waterfall for a harbor
Full of light boats that is there
Performing for thousands of people
In clothes some with places to go
Or games. Sometimes over the pillar
Of square stones its impact
Makes a light print.

So going around cities
To get to other places you found
It all on paper but the land
Was made of paper processed
To look like ferns, mud or other
Whose sea unrolled its magic
Distances and then rolled them up
Its secret was only a pocket
After all but some corners are darker
Than these moonless nights spent as on a raft

In the seclusion of a melody heard
As though through trees
And you can never ignite their touch
Long but there were homes
Flung far out near the asperities
Of a sharp, rocky pinnacle
And other collective places
Shadows of vineyards whose wine
Tasted of the forest floor
Fisheries and oyster beds
Tides under the pole
Seminaries of instruction, public
Places for electric light
And the major tax assessment area
Wrinkled on the plan
Of election to public office
Sixty-two years old bath and breakfast
The formal traffic, shadows
To make it not worth joining
After the ox had pulled away the cart.

Your plan was to separate the enemy into two groups
With the razor-edged mountains between.
It worked well on paper
But their camp had grown
To be the mountains and the map
Carefully peeled away and not torn
Was the light, a tender but tough bark
On everything. Fortunately the war was solved
In another way by isolating the two sections
Of the enemy's navy so that the mainland
Warded away the big floating ships.
Light bounced off the ends
Of the small gray waves to tell
Them in the observatory
About the great drama that was being won
To turn off the machinery
And quietly move among the rustic landscape
Scooping snow off the mountains rinsing

The coarser ones that love had
Slowly risen in the night to overflow
Wetting pillow and petal
Determined to place the letter
On the unassassinated president's desk
So that a stamp could reproduce all this
In detail, down to the last autumn leaf
And the affliction of June ride
Slowly out into the sun-blackened landscape.

Last Month

No changes of support—only
Patches of gray, here where sunlight fell.
The house seems heavier
Now that they have gone away.
In fact it emptied in record time.
When the flat table used to result
A match recedes, slowly, into the night.
The academy of the future is
Opening its doors and willing
The fruitless sunlight streams into domes,
The chairs piled high with books and papers.

The sedate one is this month's skittish one
Confirming the property that,
A timeless value, has changed hands.
And you could have a new automobile
Ping pong set and garage, but the thief
Stole everything like a miracle.
In his book there was a picture of treason only
And in the garden, cries and colors.

Civilization and Its Discontents

A people chained to aurora
I alone disarming you

Millions of facts of distributed light

Helping myself with some big boxes
Up the steps, then turning to no neighborhood;
The child's psalm, slightly sung
In the hall rushing into the small room.
Such fire! leading away from destruction.
Somewhere in outer ether I glimpsed you
Coming at me, the solo barrier did it this time,
Guessing us staying, true to be at the blue mark
Of the threshold. Tired of planning it again and again,
The cool boy distant, and the soaked-up
Afterthought, like so much rain, or roof.

The miracle took you in beside him.
Leaves rushed the window, there was clear water and the sound
    of a lock.
Now I never see you much any more.
The summers are much colder than they used to be
In that other time, when you and I were young.
I miss the human truth of your smile,
The halfhearted gaze of your palms,
And all things together, but there is no comic reign
Only the facts you put to me. You must not, then,
Be very surprised if I am alone: it is all for you,
The night, and the stars, and the way we used to be.

There is no longer any use in harping on
The incredible principle of daylong silence, the dark sunlight
As only the grass is beginning to know it,
The wreath of the north pole,
Festoons for the late return, the shy pensioners
Agasp on the lamplit air. What is agreeable
Is to hold your hand. The gravel
Underfoot. The time is for coming close. Useless
Verbs shooting the other words far away.

14

I had already swallowed the poison
And could only gaze into the distance at my life
Like a saint's with each day distinct.
No heaviness in the upland pastures. Nothing
In the forest. Only life under the huge trees
Like a coat that has grown too big, moving far away,
Cutting swamps for men like lapdogs, holding its own,
Performing once again, for you and for me.

If the Birds Knew

It is better this year.
And the clothes they wear
In the gray unweeded sky of our earth
There is no possibility of change
Because all of the true fragments are here.
So I was glad of the fog's
Taking me to you
Undetermined summer thing eaten
Of grief and passage—where you stay.
The wheel is ready to turn again.
When you have gone it will light up,
The shadow of the spokes to drown
Your departure where the summer knells
Speak to grown dawn.
There is after all a kind of promise
To the affair of the waiting weather.
We have learned not to be tired
Among the lanterns of this year of sleep
But someone pays—no transparency
Has ever hardened us before
To long piers of silence, and hedges
Of understanding, difficult passing
From one lesson to the next and the coldness
Of the consistency of our lives'
Devotion to immaculate danger.
A leaf would have settled the disturbance
Of the atmosphere, but at that high
Valley's point disbanded
Clouds that rocks smote newly
The person or persons involved
Parading slowly through the sunlit fields
Not only as though the danger did not exist
But as though the birds were in on the secret.

Far from the Rappahannock, the silent
Danube moves along toward the sea.
The brown and green Nile rolls slowly
Like the Niagara's welling descent.
Tractors stood on the green banks of the Loire
Near where it joined the Cher.
The St. Lawrence prods among black stones
And mud. But the Arno is all stones.
Wind ruffles the Hudson's
Surface. The Irawaddy is overflowing.
But the yellowish, gray Tiber
Is contained within steep banks. The Isar
Flows too fast to swim in, the Jordan's water
Courses over the flat land. The Allegheny and its boats
Were dark blue. The Moskowa is
Gray boats. The Amstel flows slowly.
Leaves fall into the Connecticut as it passes
Underneath. The Liffey is full of sewage,
Like the Seine, but unlike
The brownish-yellow Dordogne.
Mountains hem in the Colorado
And the Oder is very deep, almost
As deep as the Congo is wide.
The plain banks of the Neva are
Gray. The dark Saône flows silently.
And the Volga is long and wide
As it flows across the brownish land. The Ebro
Is blue, and slow. The Shannon flows
Swiftly between its banks. The Mississippi
Is one of the world's longest rivers, like the Amazon.
It has the Missouri for a tributary.
The Harlem flows amid factories
And buildings. The Nelson is in Canada,
Flowing. Through hard banks the Dubawnt
Forces its way. People walk near the Trent.
The landscape around the Mohawk stretches away ;
The Rubicon is merely a brook.
In winter the Main
Surges ; the Rhine sings its eternal song.

The Rhône slogs along through whitish banks
And the Rio Grande spins tales of the past.
The Loir bursts its frozen shackles
But the Moldau's wet mud ensnares it.
The East catches the light.
Near the Escaut the noise of factories echoes
And the sinuous Humboldt gurgles wildly.
The Po too flows, and the many-colored
Thames. Into the Atlantic Ocean
Pours the Garonne. Few ships navigate
On the Housatonic, but quite a few can be seen
On the Elbe. For centuries
The Afton has flowed.
                    If the Rio Negro
Could abandon its song, and the Magdalena
The jungle flowers, the Tagus
Would still flow serenely, and the Ohio
Abrade its slate banks. The tan Euphrates would
Sidle silently across the world. The Yukon
Was choked with ice, but the Susquehanna still pushed
Bravely along. The Dee caught the day's last flares
Like the Pilcomayo's carrion rose.
The Peace offered eternal fragrance
Perhaps, but the Mackenzie churned livid mud
Like tan chalk-marks. Near where
The Brahmaputra slapped swollen dikes
Was an opening through which the Limmat
Could have trickled. A young man strode the Churchill's
Banks, thinking of night. The Vistula seized
The shadows. The Theiss, stark mad, bubbled
In the windy evening. And the Ob shuffled
Crazily along. Fat billows encrusted the Dniester's
Pallid flood, and the Fraser's porous surface.
Fish gasped amid the Spree's reeds. A boat
Descended the bobbing Orinoco. When the
Marne flowed by the plants nodded
And above the glistering Gila
A sunset as beautiful as the Athabasca
Stammered. The Zambezi chimed. The Oxus

18

Flowed somewhere. The Parnahyba
Is flowing, like the wind-washed Cumberland.
The Araguía flows in the rain.
And, through overlying rocks the Isère
Cascades gently. The Guadalquiver sputtered.
Someday time will confound the Indre,
Making a rill of the Hwang. And
The Potomac rumbles softly. Crested birds
Watch the Ucayali go
Through dreaming night. You cannot stop
The Yenisei. And afterwards
The White flows strongly to its . . .
Goal. If the Tyne's shores
Hold you, and the Albany
Arrest your development, can you resist the Red's
Musk, the Meuse's situation?
A particle of mud in the Neckar
Does not turn it black. You cannot
Like the Saskatchewan, nor refuse
The meandering Yangtze, unleash
The Genesee. Does the Scamander
Still irrigate crimson plains? And the Durance
And the Pechora? The São Francisco
Skulks amid gray, rubbery nettles. The Liard's
Reflexes are slow, and the Arkansas erodes
Anthracite hummocks. The Paraná stinks.
The Ottawa is light emerald green
Among grays. Better that the Indus fade
In steaming sands! Let the Brazos
Freeze solid! And the Wabash turn to a leaden
Cinder of ice! The Marañón is too tepid, we must
Find a way to freeze it hard. The Ural
Is freezing slowly in the blasts. The black Yonne
Congeals nicely. And the Petit-Morin
Curls up on the solid earth. The Inn
Does not remember better times, and the Merrimack's
Galvanized. The Ganges is liquid snow by now;
The Vyatka's ice-gray. The once-molten Tennessee's
Curdled. The Japurá is a pack of ice. Gelid

The Columbia's gray loam banks. The Don's merely
A giant icicle. The Niger freezes, slowly.
The interminable Lena plods on
But the Purus' mercurial waters are icy, grim
With cold. The Loing is choked with fragments of ice.
The Weser is frozen, like liquid air.
And so is the Kama. And the beige, thickly flowing
Tocantins. The rivers bask in the cold.
The stern Uruguay chafes its banks,
A mass of ice. The Hooghly is solid
Ice. The Adour is silent, motionless.
The lovely Tigris is nothing but scratchy ice
Like the Yellowstone, with its osier-clustered banks.
The Mekong is beginning to thaw out a little
And the Donets gurgles beneath the
Huge blocks of ice. The Manzanares gushes free.
The Illinois darts through the sunny air again.
But the Dnieper is still ice-bound. Somewhere
The Salado propels its floes, but the Roosevelt's
Frozen. The Oka is frozen solider
Than the Somme. The Minho slumbers
In winter, nor does the Snake
Remember August. Hilarious, the Canadian
Is solid ice. The Madeira slavers
Across the thawing fields, and the Plata laughs.
The Dvina soaks up the snow. The Sava's
Temperature is above freezing. The Avon
Carols noiselessly. The Drôme presses
Grass banks; the Adige's frozen
Surface is like gray pebbles.

Birds circle the Ticino. In winter
The Var was dark blue, unfrozen. The
Thwaite, cold, is choked with sandy ice;
The Ardèche glistens feebly through the freezing rain.

The Ecclesiast

"Worse than the sunflower," she had said.
But the new dimension of truth had only recently
Burst in on us. Now it was to be condemned.
And in vagrant shadow her mothball truth is eaten.
In cool, like-it-or-not shadow the humdrum is consumed.
Tired housewives begat it some decades ago,
A small piece of truth that if it was honey to the lips
Was also millions of miles from filling the place reserved for it.
You see how honey crumbles your universe
Which seems like an institution—how many walls?

Then everything, in her belief, was to be submerged
And soon. There was no life you could live out to its end
And no attitude which, in the end, would save you.
The monkish and the frivolous alike were to be trapped
          in death's capacious claw
But listen while I tell you about the wallpaper—
There was a key to everything in that oak forest
But a sad one. Ever since childhood there
Has been this special meaning to everything.
You smile at your friend's joke, but only later, through tears.

For the shoe pinches, even though it fits perfectly.
Apples were made to be gathered, also the whole host of the
          world's ailments and troubles.
There is no time like the present for giving in to this temptation.
Tomorrow you'll weep—what of it? There is time enough
Once the harvest is in and the animals put away for the winter
To stand at the uncomprehending window cultivating the desert
With salt tears which will never do anyone any good.
My dearest I am as a galleon on salt billows.
Perfume my head with forgetting all about me.

For some day these projects will return.
The funereal voyage over ice-strewn seas is ended.
You wake up forgetting. Already
Daylight shakes you in the yard.
The hands remain empty. They are constructing an osier basket
Just now, and across the sunlight darkness is taking root anew

In intense activity. You shall never have seen it just this way
And that is to be your one reward.

Fine vapors escape from whatever is doing the living.
The night is cold and delicate and full of angels
Pounding down the living. The factories are all lit up,
The chime goes unheard.
We are together at last, though far apart.

Perhaps we ought to feel with more imagination.
As today the sky 70 degrees above zero with lines falling
The way September moves a lace curtain to be near a pear,
The oddest device can't be usual. And that is where
The pejorative sense of fear moves axles. In the stars
There is no longer any peace, emptied like a cup of coffee
Between the blinding rain that interviews.

You were my quintuplets when I decided to leave you
Opening a picture book the pictures were all of grass
Slowly the book was on fire, you the reader
Sitting with specs full of smoke exclaimed
How it was a rhyme for "brick" or "redder."
The next chapter told all about a brook.
You were beginning to see the relation when a tidal wave
Arrived with sinking ships that spelled out "Aladdin."
I thought about the Arab boy in his cave
But the thoughts came faster than advice.
If you knew that snow was a still toboggan in space
The print could rhyme with "fallen star."

The Thousand Islands

Keeping warm now, while it lasts
In the life we must suppose, continuance
Quickens the scrap which falls to us.

Painless rigors, like thistledown,
Strapped to us like a heavy pack
The massed air hanging above.

The tether of you to this bank
To understand the flesh left splinters.
Depths of understanding preside
Shelving steeply into a kind of flow
Stumble happily as through a miracle
Opening around you
Pinned to the moment.
Your eyes reflect a hunting scene.

A promise of so much that is to come,
Extracted, accepted gladly
But within its narrow limits
No knowledge yet, nothing which can be used.

You are grateful for the imaginary pause.

No one had imagined that the storm would be like this
To discover its heart. The blind enemy
Exalting the possibility of defeat
Behind glass first unthinkable then not so much
It would be better if one smile
The one successful day drew darkness from the folds around it.
Meadows then might melt into something
For play, the necessity gone. But your
Idea is not continuing—a swift imperfect
Condensation of the indifference you feel
To be the worn fiber and bone which must surround you
For the permanence of what's already happened in you.

Blackness plays no part; the eye
Is black but there is no depth.

It is the surface black which attacks the shape.
Bending it to present uses.
The face on the door a hundred million years old
Slightly smaller than real life
To accept the cold air and bread
And cause, in the distance, an old satisfaction.

Their simplest construction rising slowly toward
Your neutral ceiling in which are capsized
Forever afternoon smells and rich zero disturbance
As you unharness the horse moves slowly back
Changing too the position escapes you mild and drawn

And prisons think restlessly shifting
There are ever new arrivals
New standard of living and expunging
With a shout something you'd rather have

These equators fixed you'd esteemed
The discovery
Only lacking to fail eagerly
The approach of the cool marble subject
An aphrodisiac in its tall gray flowering
Into separate lengths later lost
Brought down with it hesitancy
The bent clouds' arrow and rutted woods.
At Pine Creek imitation the circle
Had swallowed the useless mystery again
As clouds reappear after rains.

A Blessing in Disguise

Yes, they are alive and can have those colors,
But I, in my soul, am alive too.
I feel I must sing and dance, to tell
Of this in a way, that knowing you may be drawn to me.

And I sing amid despair and isolation
Of the chance to know you, to sing of me
Which are you. You see,
You hold me up to the light in a way

I should never have expected, or suspected, perhaps
Because you always tell me I am you,
And right. The great spruces loom.
I am yours to die with, to desire.

I cannot ever think of me, I desire you
For a room in which the chairs ever
Have their backs turned to the light
Inflicted on the stone and paths, the real trees

That seem to shine at me through a lattice toward you.
If the wild light of this January day is true
I pledge me to be truthful unto you
Whom I cannot ever stop remembering.

Remembering to forgive. Remember to pass beyond you into
        the day
On the wings of the secret you will never know.
Taking me from myself, in the path
Which the pastel girth of the day has assigned to me.

I prefer "you" in the plural, I want "you,"
You must come to me, all golden and pale
Like the dew and the air.
And then I start getting this feeling of exaltation.

Clepsydra

Hasn't the sky? Returned from moving the other
Authority recently dropped, wrested as much of
That severe sunshine as you need now on the way
You go. The reason why it happened only since
You woke up is letting the steam disappear
From those clouds when the landscape all around
Is hilly sites that will have to be reckoned
Into the total for there to be more air: that is,
More fitness read into the undeduced result, than land.
This means never getting any closer to the basic
Principle operating behind it than to the distracted
Entity of a mirage. The half-meant, half-perceived
Motions of fronds out of idle depths that are
Summer. And expansion into little draughts.
The reply wakens easily, darting from
Untruth to willed moment, scarcely called into being
Before it swells, the way a waterfall
Drums at different levels. Each moment
Of utterance is the true one; likewise none are true,
Only is the bounding from air to air, a serpentine
Gesture which hides the truth behind a congruent
Message, the way air hides the sky, is, in fact,
Tearing it limb from limb this very moment: but
The sky has pleaded already and this is about
As graceful a kind of non-absence as either
Has a right to expect: whether it's the form of
Some creator who has momentarily turned away,
Marrying detachment with respect, so that the pieces
Are seen as parts of a spectrum, independent
Yet symbolic of their spaced-out times of arrival;
Whether on the other hand all of it is to be
Seen as no luck. A recurring whiteness like
The face of stone pleasure, urging forward as
Nostrils what only meant dust. But the argument,
That is its way, has already left these behind: it
Is, it would have you believe, the white din up ahead
That matters: unformed yells, rocketings,
Affected turns, and tones of voice called
By upper shadows toward some cloud of belief

Or its unstated circumference. But the light
Has already gone from there too and it may be that
It is lines contracting into a plane. We hear so much
Of its further action that at last it seems that
It is we, our taking it into account rather, that are
The reply that prompted the question, and
That the latter, like a person waking on a pillow
Has the sensation of having dreamt the whole thing,
Of returning to participate in that dream, until
The last word is exhausted; certainly this is
Peace of a sort, like nets drying in the sun,
That we must progress toward the whole thing
About an hour ago. As long as it is there
You will desire it as its tag of wall sinks
Deeper as though hollowed by sunlight that
Just fits over it; it is both mirage and the little
That was present, the miserable totality
Mustered at any given moment, like your eyes
And all they speak of, such as your hands, in lost
Accents beyond any dream of ever wanting them again.
To have this to be constantly coming back from—
Nothing more, really, than surprise at your absence
And preparing to continue the dialogue into
Those mysterious and near regions that are
Precisely the time of its being furthered.
Seeing it, as it was, dividing that time,
Casting colored paddles against the welter
Of a future of disunion just to abolish confusion
And permit level walks into the gaze of its standing
Around admiringly, it was then, that it was these
Moments that were the truth, although each tapered
Into the distant surrounding night. But
Wasn't it their blindness, instead, and wasn't this
The fact of being so turned in on each other that
Neither would ever see his way clear again? It
Did not stagger the imagination so long as it stayed
This way, comparable to exclusion from the light of the stars
That drenched every instant of that being, in an egoistic way,
As though their round time were only the reverse

Of some more concealable, vengeful purpose to become known
Once its result had more or less established
The look of the horizon. But the condition
Of those moments of timeless elasticity and blindness
Was being joined secretly so
That their paths would cross again and be separated
Only to join again in a final assumption rising like a shout
And be endless in the discovery of the declamatory
Nature of the distance traveled. All this is
Not without small variations and surprises, yet
An invisible fountain continually destroys and
        refreshes the previsions.
Then is their permanence merely a function of
The assurance with which it's understood, assurance
Which, you might say, goes a long way toward conditioning
Whatever result? But there was no statement
At the beginning. There was only a breathless waste,
A dumb cry shaping everything in projected
After-effects orphaned by playing the part intended for them,
Though one must not forget that the nature of this
Emptiness, these previsions,
Was that it could only happen here, on this page held
Too close to be legible, sprouting erasures, except that they
Ended everything in the transparent sphere of what was
Intended only a moment ago, spiraling further out, its
Gesture finally dissolving in the weather.
It was the long way back out of sadness
Of that first meeting: a half-triumph, an imaginary feeling
Which still protected its events and pauses, the way
A telescope protects its view of distant mountains
And all they include, the coming and going,
Moving correctly up to other levels, preparing to spend the night
There where the tiny figures halt as darkness comes on,
Beside some loud torrent in an empty yet personal
Landscape, which has the further advantage of being
What surrounds without insisting, the very breath so
Honorably offered, and accepted in the same spirit.
There was in fact pleasure in those high walls.
Each moment seemed to bore back into the centuries

29

For profit and manners, and an old way of looking that
Continually shaped those lips into a smile. Or it was
Like standing at the edge of a harbor early on a summer morning
With the discreet shadows cast by the water all around
And a feeling, again, of emptiness, but of richness in the way
The whole thing is organized, on what a miraculous scale,
Really what is meant by a human level, with the figures of giants
Not too much bigger than the men who have come to
        petition them:
A moment that gave not only itself, but
Also the means of keeping it, of not turning to dust
Or gestures somewhere up ahead
But of becoming complicated like the torrent
In new dark passages, tears and laughter which
Are a sign of life, of distant life in this case.
And yet, as always happens, there would come a moment when
Acts no longer sufficed and the calm
Of this true progression hardened into shreds
Of another kind of calm, returning to the conclusion, its premises
Undertaken before any formal agreement had been reached, hence
A writ that was the shadow of the colossal reason behind all this
Like a second, rigid body behind the one you know is yours.
And it was in vain that tears blotted the contract now, because
It had been freely drawn up and consented to as insurance
Against the very condition it was now so efficiently
Seeking to establish. It had reduced that other world,
The round one of the telescope, to a kind of very fine
        powder or dust
So small that space could not remember it.
Thereafter any signs of feeling were cut short by
The comfort and security, a certain elegance even,
Like the fittings of a ship, that are after all
The most normal things in the world. Yes, perhaps, but the words
"After all" are important for understanding the almost
Exaggerated strictness of the condition, and why, in spite of this,
It seemed the validity of the former continuing was
Not likely to be reinstated for a long time.
"After all," that too might be possible, as indeed
All kinds of things are possible in the widening angle of

30

The day, as it comes to blush with pleasure and increase,
So that light sinks into itself, becomes dark and heavy
Like a surface stained with ink: there was something
Not quite good or correct about the way
Things were looking recently: hadn't the point
Of all this new construction been to provide
A protected medium for the exchanges each felt of such vital
Concern, and wasn't it now giving itself the airs of a palace?
And yet her hair had never been so long.
It was a feeling of well-being, if you will, as though a smallest
Distant impulse had rendered the whole surface ultra-sensitive
But its fierceness was still acquiescence
To the nature of this goodness already past
And it was a kind of sweet acknowledgment of how
The past is yours, to keep invisible if you wish
But also to make absurd elaborations with
And in this way prolong your dance of non-discovery
In brittle, useless architecture that is nevertheless
The map of your desires, irreproachable, beyond
Madness and the toe of approaching night, if only
You desire to arrange it this way. Your acts
Are sentinels against this quiet
Invasion. Long may you prosper, and may your years
Be the throes of what is even now exhausting itself
In one last effort to outwit us; it could only be a map
Of the world: in their defeat such peninsulas as become
Prolongations of our reluctance to approach, but also
Fine days on whose memorable successions of events
We shall be ever afterwards tempted to dwell. I am
Not speaking of a partially successful attempt to be
Opposite; anybody at all can read that page, it has only
To be thrust in front of him. I mean now something much broader,
The sum total of all the private aspects that can ever
Become legible in what is outside, as much in the rocks
And foliage as in the invisible look of the distant
Ether and in the iron fist that suddenly closes over your own.
I see myself in this totality, and meanwhile
I am only a transparent diagram, of manners and
Private words with the certainty of being about to fall.

31

And even this crumb of life I also owe to you
For being so close as to seal out knowledge of that other
Voluntary life, and so keep its root in darkness until your
Maturity when your hair will actually be the branches
Of a tree with the light pouring through them.
It intensifies echoes in such a way as to
Form a channel to absorb every correct motion.
In this way any direction taken was the right one,
Leading first to you, and through you to
Myself that is beyond you and which is the same thing as space,
That is the stammering vehicles that remain unknown,
Eating the sky in all sincerity because the difference
Can never be made up: therefore, why not examine the distance?
It seemed he had been repeating the same stupid phrase
Over and over throughout his life; meanwhile
Infant destinies had suavely matured; there was
To be a meeting or collection of them that very evening.
He was out of it of course for having lain happily awake
On the tepid fringes of that field or whatever
Whose center was beginning to churn darkly, but even more
        for having
The progression of minutes by accepting them, as one accepts
        drops of rain
As they form a shower, and without worrying about the fine
        weather that will come after.
Why shouldn't all climate and all music be equal
Without growing? There should be an invariable balance of
Contentment to hold everything in place, ministering
To stunted memories, helping them stand alone
And return into the world, without ever looking back at
What they might have become, even though in doing so they
Might just once have been the truth that, invisible,
Still surrounds us like the air and is the dividing force
Between our slightest steps and the notes taken on them.
It is because everything is relative
That we shall never see in that sphere of pure wisdom and
Entertainment much more than groping shadows of an incomplete
Former existence so close it burns like the mouth that
Closes down over all your effort like the moment

Of death, but stays, raging and burning the design of
Its intentions into the house of your brain, until
You wake up alone, the certainty that it
Wasn't a dream your only clue to why the walls
Are turning on you and why the windows no longer speak
Of time but are themselves, transparent guardians you
Invented for what there was to hide. Which has now
Grown up, or moved away, as a jewel
Exists when there is no one to look at it, and this
Existence saps your own. Perhaps you are being kept here
Only so that somewhere else the peculiar light of someone's
Purpose can blaze unexpectedly in the acute
Angles of the rooms. It is not a question, then,
Of having not lived in vain. What is meant is that this distant
Image of you, the way you really are, is the test
Of how you see yourself, and regardless of whether or not
You hesitate, it may be assumed that you have won, that this
Wooden and external representation
Returns the full echo of what you meant
With nothing left over, from that circumference now alight
With ex-possibilities become present fact, and you
Must wear them like clothing, moving in the shadow of
Your single and twin existence, waking in intact
Appreciation of it, while morning is still and before the body
Is changed by the faces of evening.

The Skaters

I

These decibels
Are a kind of flagellation, an entity of sound
Into which being enters, and is apart.
Their colors on a warm February day
Make for masses of inertia, and hips
Prod out of the violet-seeming into a new kind
Of demand that stumps the absolute because not new
In the sense of the next one in an infinite series
But, as it were, pre-existing or pre-seeming in
Such a way as to contrast funnily with the unexpectedness
And somehow push us all into perdition.

Here a scarf flies, there an excited call is heard.

The answer is that it is novelty
That guides these swift blades o'er the ice
Projects into a finer expression (but at the expense
Of energy) the profile I cannot remember.
Colors slip away from and chide us. The human mind
Cannot retain anything except perhaps the dismal two-note theme
Of some sodden "dump" or lament.

But the water surface ripples, the whole light changes.

We children are ashamed of our bodies
But we laugh and, demanded, talk of sex again
And all is well. The waves of morning harshness
Float away like coal-gas into the sky.
But how much survives? How much of any one of us survives?
The articles we'd collect—stamps of the colonies
With greasy cancellation marks, mauve, magenta and chocolate,
Or funny-looking dogs we'd see in the street, or bright remarks.
One collects bullets. An Indianapolis, Indiana man collects
        slingshots of all epochs, and so on.

Subtracted from our collections, though, these go on a little
        while, collecting aimlessly. We still support them.
But so little energy they have! And up the swollen sands
Staggers the darkness fiend, with the storm fiend close behind him!

34

True, melodious tolling does go on in that awful pandemonium,
Certain resonances are not utterly displeasing to the
        terrified eardrum.
Some paroxysms are dinning of tambourine, others suggest piano
        room or organ loft
For the most dissonant night charms us, even after death. This,
        after all, may be happiness: tuba notes awash on the great
        flood, ruptures of xylophone, violins, limpets, grace-notes,
        the musical instrument called serpent, viola da gambas,
        aeolian harps, clavicles, pinball machines, electric drills, que
        sais-je encore!
The performance has rapidly reached your ear; silent and tear-
        stained, in the post-mortem shock, you stand listening, awash
With memories of hair in particular, part of the welling that is you,
The gurgling of harp, cymbal, glockenspiel, triangle, temple block,
        English horn and metronome! And still no presentiment, no
        feeling of pain before or after.
The passage sustains, does not give. And you have come far indeed.

Yet to go from "not interesting" to "old and uninteresting,"
To be surrounded by friends, though late in life,
To hear the wings of the spirit, though far . . . .
Why do I hurriedly undrown myself to cut you down?
"I am yesterday," and my fault is eternal.
I do not expect constant attendance, knowing myself
        insufficient for your present demands
And I have a dim intuition that I am that other "I" with which
        we began.
My cheeks as blank walls to your tears and eagerness
Fondling that other, as though you had let him get away forever.

The evidence of the visual henceforth replaced
By the great shadow of trees falling over life.

A child's devotion
To this normal, shapeless entity . . . .

Forgotten as the words fly briskly across, each time
Bringing down meaning as snow from a low sky, or rabbits

35

flushed from a wood.
How strange that the narrow perspective lines
Always seem to meet, although parallel, and that an insane
        ghost could do this,
Could make the house seem so much farther in the distance, as
It seemed to the horse, dragging the sledge of a perspective line.
Dim banners in the distance, to die . . . . And nothing put to
        rights. The pigs in their cages

And so much snow, but it is to be littered with waste and ashes
So that cathedrals may grow. Out of this spring builds a tolerable
Affair of brushwood, the sea is felt behind oak wands,
        noiselessly pouring.
Spring with its promise of winter, and the black ivy once again
On the porch, its yellow perspective bands in place
And the horse nears them and weeps.

So much has passed through my mind this morning
That I can give you but a dim account of it:
It is already after lunch, the men are returning to their
        positions around the cement mixer
And I try to sort out what has happened to me. The bundle
        of Gerard's letters,
And that awful bit of news buried on the back page of
        yesterday's paper.
Then the news of you this morning, in the snow.
        Sometimes the interval
Of bad news is so brisk that . . . And the human brain, with its
        tray of images
Seems a sorcerer's magic lantern, projecting black and orange
        cellophane shadows
On the distance of my hand . . . The very reaction's puny,
And when we seek to move around, wondering what our position
        is now, what the arm of that chair.

A great wind lifted these cardboard panels
Horizontal in the air. At once the perspective with the horse
Disappeared in a **bigarrure** of squiggly lines. The image with
        the crocodile in it became no longer apparent.

36

Thus a great wind cleanses, as a new ruler
Edits new laws, sweeping the very breath of the streets
Into posterior trash. The films have changed—
The great titles on the scalloped awning have turned dry and
    blight-colored.
No wind that does not penetrate a man's house, into the very
    bowels of the furnace,
Scratching in dust a name on the mirror—say, and what
    about letters,
The dried grasses, fruits of the winter—gosh! Everything
    is trash!
The wind points to the advantages of decay
At the same time as removing them far from the sight of men.
The regent of the winds, Aeolus, is a symbol for all
    earthly potentates
Since holding this sickening, festering process by which
    we are cleansed
Of afterthought.
                A girl slowly descended the line of steps.

The wind and treason are partners, turning secrets over to
    the military police.

Lengthening arches. The intensity of minor acts.
    As skaters elaborate their distances,
Taking a separate line to its end. Returning to the mass,
    they join each other
Blotted in an incredible mess of dark colors, and again
    reappearing to take the theme
Some little distance, like fishing boats developing from the
    land different parabolas,
Taking the exquisite theme far, into farness, to Land's End,
    to the ends of the earth!

But the livery of the year, the changing air
Bring each to fulfillment. Leaving phrases unfinished,
Gestures half-sketched against woodsmoke. The abundant sap
Oozes in girls' throats, the sticky words, half-uttered,
    unwished for,

A blanket disbelief, quickly supplanted by idle questions
      that fade in turn.
Slowly the mood turns to look at itself as some urchin
Forgotten by the roadside. New schemes are got up, new taxes,
Earthworks. And the hours becomes light again.
Girls wake up in it.

It is best to remain indoors. Because there is error
In so much precision. As flames are fanned, wishful
      thinking arises
Bearing its own prophets, its pointed ignoring.
      And just as a desire
Settles down at the end of a long spring day, over heather
      and watered shoot and dried rush field,
So error is plaited into desires not yet born.

Therefore the post must be resumed (is being falsified
To be forever involved, tragically, with one's own image?).
The studio light suddenly invaded the long
      casement—values were what
She knows now. But the floor is being slowly pulled apart
Like straw under those limpid feet.
And Helga, in the minuscule apartment in Jersey City
Is reacting violet to the same kind of dress, is drawing death
Again in blossoms against the reactionary fire ... pulsing
And knowing nothing to superb lambent distances that intercalate
This city. Is the death of the cube repeated. Or in the
      musical album.

It is time now for a general understanding of
The meaning of all this. The meaning of Helga, importance
      of the setting, etc.
A description of the blues. Labels on bottles
And all kinds of discarded objects that ought to be described.
But can one ever be sure of which ones?
Isn't this a death-trap, wanting to put too much in
So the floor sags, as under the weight of a piano,
      or a piano-legged girl
And the whole house of cards comes dinning down around
      one's ears!

38

But this is an important aspect of the question
Which I am not ready to discuss, am not at all ready to,
This leaving-out business. On it hinges the very importance
     of what's novel
Or autocratic, or dense or silly. It is as well to call attention
To it by exaggeration, perhaps. But calling attention
Isn't the same thing as explaining, and as I said I am not ready
To line phrases with the costly stuff of explanation, and shall not,
Will not do so for the moment. Except to say that the carnivorous
Way of these lines is to devour their own nature, leaving
Nothing but a bitter impression of absence, which as we know
     involves presence, but still.
Nevertheless these are fundamental absences, struggling to
     get up and be off themselves.

This, thus is a portion of the subject of this poem
Which is in the form of falling snow:
That is, the individual flakes are not essential to the
     importance of the whole's becoming so much of a truism
That their importance is again called in question, to be
     denied further out, and again and again like this.
Hence, neither the importance of the individual flake,
Nor the importance of the whole impression of the storm,
     if it has any, is what it is,
But the rhythm of the series of repeated jumps, from
     abstract into positive and back to a slightly less
     diluted abstract.

Mild effects are the result.

I cannot think any more of going out into all that, will stay here
With my quiet **schmerzen**. Besides the storm is almost over
Having frozen the face of the bust into a strange style with the lips
And the teeth the most distinct part of the whole business.

It is this madness to explain . . . .

What is the matter with plain old-fashioned cause-and-effect?
Leaving one alone with romantic impressions of the trees, the sky?

39

Who, actually, is going to be fooled one instant by these
        phony explanations,
Think them important? So back we go to the old,
        imprecise feelings, the
Common knowledge, the importance of duly suffering and
        the occasional glimpses
Of some balmy felicity. The world of Schubert's lieder.
        I am fascinated
Though by the urge to get out of it all, by going
Further in and correcting the whole mismanaged mess.
        But am afraid I'll
Be of no help to you. Good-bye.

As balloons are to the poet, so to the ground
Its varied assortment of trees. The more assorted they are, the
Vaster his experience. Sometimes
You catch sight of them on a level with the top story of a house,
Strung up there for publicity purposes. Or like those bubbles
Children make with a kind of ring, not a pipe, and probably
        using some detergent
Rather than plain everyday soap and water. Where was I?
        The balloons
Drift thoughtfully over the land, not exactly commenting on it;
These are the range of the poet's experience. He can hide in trees
Like a hamadryad, but wisely prefers not to, letting the balloons
Idle him out of existence, as a car idles. Traveling faster
And more furiously across unknown horizons, belted into the night
Wishing more and more to be unlike someone, getting the
        whole thing
(So he believes) out of his system. Inventing systems.
We are a part of some system, thinks he, just as the sun is part of
The solar system. Trees brake his approach. And he seems
        to be wearing but
Half a coat, viewed from one side. A "half-man" look
        inspiring the disgust of honest folk
Returning from chores, the milk frozen, the pump heaped high
        with a chapeau of snow,
The "No Skating" sign as well. But it is here that he is best,
Face to face with the unsmiling alternatives of his nerve-wracking

existence.
Placed squarely in front of his dilemma, on all fours before the
    lamentable spectacle of the unknown.
Yet knowing where men **are** coming from. It is this, to hold the
    candle up to the album.

II

Under the window marked "General Delivery" . . .

This should be a letter
Throwing you a minute to one side,
Of how this tossing looks harmonious from a distance,
Like sea or the tops of trees, and how
Only when one gets closer is its sadness small and appreciable.
It can be held in the hand.

All this must go into a letter.
Also the feeling of being lived, looking for people,
And gradual peace and relaxation.

But there's no personal involvement:
These sudden bursts of hot and cold
Are wreathed in shadowless intensity
Whose moment saps them of all characteristics.
Thus beginning to rest you at once know.

Once there was a point in these islands,
Coming to see where the rock had rotted away,
And turning into a tiny speck in the distance.

But war's savagery. . . . Even the most patient scholar, now
Could hardly reconstruct the old fort exactly as it was.
That trees continue to wave over it. That there is also a small
    museum somewhere inside.
That the history of costume is no less fascinating than the
    history of great migrations.
I'd like to bugger you all up,
Deliberately falsify all your old suck-ass notions

41

Of how chivalry is being lived. What goes on in beehives.
But the whole filthy mess, misunderstandings included,
Problems about the tunic button etc. How much of any
    one person is there.

Still, after bananas and spoonbread in the shadow of the
    old walls
It is cooling to return under the eaves in the shower
That probably fell while we were inside, examining bowknots,
Old light-bulb sockets, places where the whitewash had begun
    to flake
With here and there an old map or illustration. Here's one for
    instance—
Looks like a weather map . . . or a coiled bit of wallpaper
    with a design
Of faded hollyhocks, or abstract fruit and gumdrops in chains.

But how is it that you are always indoors, peering at too
    heavily canceled stamps through a greasy magnifying
    glass?
And slowly the incoherencies of day melt in
A general wishful thinking of night
To peruse certain stars over the bay.
Cataracts of peace pour from the poised heavens
And only fear of snakes prevents us from passing the
    night in the open air.
The day is definitely at an end.

Old heavens, you used to tweak above us,
Standing like rain whenever a salvo . . . Old heavens,
You lying there above the old, but not ruined, fort,
Can you hear, there, what I am saying?

For it is you I am parodying,
Your invisible denials. And the almost correct impressions
Corroborated by newsprint, which is so fine.
I call to you there, but I do not think that you will answer me.

For I am condemned to drum my fingers

42

On the closed lid of this piano, this tedious planet, earth
As it winks to you through the aspiring, growing distances,
A last spark before the night.

There was much to be said in favor of storms
But you seem to have abandoned them in favor of endless light.
I cannot say that I think the change much of an improvement.
There is something fearful in these summer nights that go on
    forever. . . .

We are nearing the Moorish coast, I think, in a **bateau**.
I wonder if I will have any friends there
Whether the future will be kinder to me than the past, for example,
And am all set to be put out, finding it to be not.

Still, I am prepared for this voyage, and for anything else you
    may care to mention.
Not that I am not afraid, but there is very little time left.
You have probably made travel arrangements, and know the feeling.
Suddenly, one morning, the little train arrives in the station, but
    oh, so big

It is! Much bigger and faster than anyone told you.
A bewhiskered student in an old baggy overcoat is waiting to
    take it.
"Why do you want to go **there**," they all say. "It is better in the
    other direction."
And so it is. There people are free, at any rate. But where you
    are going no one is.

Still there are parks and libraries to be visited, "la Bibliothèque
    Municipale,"
Hotel reservations and all that rot. Old American films dubbed
    into the foreign language,
Coffee and whiskey and cigar stubs. Nobody minds. And rain
    on the bristly wool of your topcoat.
I realize that I never knew why I wanted to come.

Yet I shall never return to the past, that attic,

Its sailboats are perhaps more beautiful than these, these
    I am leaning against,
Spangled with diamonds and orange and purple stains,
Bearing me once again in quest of the unknown. These sails
    are life itself to me.

I heard a girl say this once, and cried, and brought her
    fresh fruit and fishes,
Olives and golden baked loaves. She dried her tears and
    thanked me.
Now we are both setting sail into the purplish evening.
I love it! This cruise can never last long enough for me.

But once more, office desks, radiators—No! That is behind me.
No more dullness, only movies and love and laughter, sex and fun.
The ticket seller is blowing his little horn—hurry before the window
    slams down.
The train we are getting onto is a boat train, and the boats
    are really boats this time.

But I heard the heavens say—Is it right? This continual
    changing back and forth?
Laughter and tears and so on? Mightn't just plain sadness be
    sufficient for him?
No! I'll not accept that any more, you bewhiskered old caverns
    of blue!
This is just right for me. I am cozily ensconced in the balcony
    of my face

Looking out over the whole darn countryside, a beacon of
    satisfaction
I am. I'll not trade places with a king. Here I am then, continuing
    but ever beginning
My perennial voyage, into new memories, new hope and flowers
The way the coasts glide past you. I shall never forget this moment

Because it consists of purest ecstasy. I am happier now than I
    ever dared believe
Anyone could be. And we finger down the dog-eared coasts . . . .

It is all passing! It is past! No, I am here,
Bellow the coasts, and even the heavens roar their assent

As we pick up a lemon-colored light horizontally
Projected into the night, the night that heaven
Was kind enough to send, and I launch into the happiest dreams,
Happier once again, because tomorrow is already here.

Yet certain kernels remain. Clouds that drift past sheds—
Read it in the official bulletin. We shan't be putting out today.
The old stove smoked worse than ever because rain was coming
    down its chimney.
Only the bleary eye of fog accosted one through the mended pane.

Outside, the swamp water lapped the broken wood step.
A rowboat was moored in the alligator-infested swamp.
Somewhere, from deep in the interior of the jungle, a groan was
    heard.
Could it be . . . ? Anyway, a rainy day—wet weather.

The whole voyage will have to be canceled.
It would be impossible to make different connections.
Anyway the hotels are all full at this season. The junks
    packed with refugees
Returning from the islands. Sea-bream and flounder abound in
    the muddied waters. . . .

They in fact represent the backbone of the island economy.
That, and cigar rolling. Please leave your papers at the desk as
    you pass out,
You know. "The Wedding March." Ah yes, that's the way. The
    couple descend
The steps of the little old church. Ribbons are flung, ribbons
    of cloud

And the sun seems to be coming out. But there have been so
    many false alarms. . . .
No, it's happened! The storm is over. Again the weather is fine
    and clear.

And the voyage? It's on! Listen everybody, the ship is starting,
I can hear its whistle's roar! We have just time enough to make
     it to the dock!

And away they pour, in the sulfurous sunlight,
To the aqua and silver waters where stands the glistening
     white ship
And into the great vessel they flood, a motley and happy crowd
Chanting and pouring down hymns on the surface of the ocean. . . .

Pulling, tugging us along with them, by means of streamers,
Golden and silver confetti. Smiling, we laugh and sing with
     the revelers
But are not quite certain that we want to go—the dock is so
     sunny and warm.
That majestic ship will pull up anchor who knows where?

And full of laughter and tears, we sidle once again with the
     other passengers.
The ground is heaving under foot. Is it the ship? It could be the
     dock. . . .
And with a great whoosh all the sails go up. . . . Hideous black
     smoke belches forth from the funnels
Smudging the gold carnival costumes with the gaiety of its
     jet-black soot

And, as into a tunnel the voyage starts
Only, as I said, to be continued. The eyes of those left
     standing on the dock are wet
But ours are dry. Into the secretive, vaporous night with all of us!
Into the unknown, the unknown that loves us, the great unknown!

So man nightly
Sparingly descends
The birches and the hay   all of him
Pruned, erect for vital contact. As the separate mists of day slip
Uncomplainingly into the atmosphere. Loving you?
     The question sinks into

46

That mazy business
About writing or to have read it in some book
To silently move away. At Gannosfonadiga the pumps
Working, argent in the thickening sunset, like boys' shoulders

And you return to the question as to a calendar of November
Again and again consulting the surface of that enormous affair
I think not to have loved you   but the music
Petting the enameled   slow-imagined stars

A concert of dissatisfaction whereby   gutter and dust seep
To engross the mirrored image and its landscape:

As when
                    through darkness and mist
                                        the pole-bringer
                                        demandingly watches
I am convinced these things are of some importance.

Firstly, it is a preparing to go outward
Of no planet limiting the enjoyment
Of motion—hips free of embarrassment etc.

The figure 8 is a perfect symbol
Of the freedom to be gained in this kind of activity.
The perspective lines of the barn are another and different
        kind of example
(Viz. "Rigg's Farm, near Aysgarth, Wensleydale," or the
        "Sketch at Norton")
In which we escape ourselves—putrefying mass of prevari-
        cations etc.—
In remaining close to the limitations imposed.

Another example is this separate dying
Still keeping in mind the coachmen, servant girls, duchesses,
        etc. (cf. Jeremy Taylor)
Falling away, rhythm of too-wet snow, but parallel
With the kind of rhythm substituting for "meaning."

Looked at from this angle the problem of death and survival
Ages slightly. For the solutions are millionfold, like
        waves of wild geese returning in spring.
Scarcely we know where to turn to avoid suffering, I mean
There are so many places.

So, coachman-servile, or scullion-slatternly, but each place is
        taken.

The lines that draw nearer together are said to "vanish."
The point where they meet is their vanishing point.

Spaces, as they recede, become smaller.

But another, more urgent question imposes itself—
        that of poverty.
How to excuse it to oneself? The wetness and coldness?
        Dirt and grime?
Uncomfortable, unsuitable lodgings, with a depressing view?
The peeled geranium flowering in a rusted tomato can,
Framed in a sickly ray of sunlight, a tragic chromo?

A broken mirror nailed up over a chipped enamel basin,
        whose turgid waters
Reflect the fly-specked calendar—with ecstatic Dutch girl
        clasping tulips—
On the far wall. Hanging from one nail, an old velvet hat
        with a tattered bit of veiling—last remnant of former finery.
The bed well made. The whole place scrupulously clean,
        but cold and damp.

All this, wedged into a pyramidal ray of light, is my own
        invention.

But to return to our tomato can—those spared by the goats
Can be made into a practical telephone, the two halves being
        connected by a length of wire.
You can talk to your friend in the next room, or around corners.

An American inventor made a fortune with just such a contraption.
The branches tear at the sky—

Things too tiny to be remembered in recorded history—the
      backfiring of a bus
In a Paris street in 1932, and all the clumsy seductions and
      amateur paintings done,
Clamber to join in the awakening
To take a further role in my determination. These clown-shapes
Filling up the available space for miles, like acres of red and
      mustard pom-poms
Dusted with a pollen we call "an air of truth." Massed mounds
Of Hades it is true. I propose a general housecleaning
Of these true and valueless shapes which pester us with their
      raisons d'être
Whom no one (that is their weakness) can ever get to like.

There are moving parts to be got out of order,
However, in the flame fountain. Add gradually one ounce, by
      measure, of sulphuric acid
To five or six ounces of water in an earthenware basin. Add
      to it, also gradually, about three-quarters of an ounce of
      granulated zinc.
A rapid production of hydrogen gas will instantly take place.
      Then add,
From time to time, a few pieces of phosphorus the size of a pea.
A multitude of gas bubbles will be produced, which will fire on
      the surface of the effervescing liquid.
The whole surface of the liquid will become luminous, and fire
      balls, with jets of fire,
Will dart from the bottom, through the fluid with great rapidity
      and a hissing noise.

Sure, but a simple shelter from this or other phenomena
      is easily contrived.

But how luminous the fountain! Its sparks seem to aspire
      to reach the sky!
And so much energy in those bubbles. A wise man could

contemplate his face in them
With impunity, but fools would surely do better not to approach
too close
Because any intense physical activity like that implies danger for
the unwary and the uneducated. Great balls of fire!
In my day we used to make "fire designs," using a saturated
solution of nitrate of potash.
Then we used to take a smooth stick, and using the solution as ink,
draw with it on sheets of white tissue paper.
Once it was thoroughly dry, the writing would be invisible.
By means of a spark from a smoldering match ignite the potas-
sium nitrate at any part of the drawing,
First laying the paper on a plate or tray in a darkened room.
The fire will smolder along the line of the invisible drawing
until the design is complete.

Meanwhile the fire fountain is still smoldering and welling
Casting off a hellish stink and wild fumes of pitch
Acrid as jealousy. And it might be
That flame writing might be visible right there, in the gaps in
the smoke
Without going through the bother of the solution-writing.
A word here and there—"promise" or "beware"—you have to
go the long way round
Before you find the entrance to that side is closed.
The phosphorescent liquid is still heaving and boiling, however.
And what if this insane activity were itself a kind of drawing
Of April sidewalks, and young trees bursting into timid leaf
And dogs sniffing hydrants, the fury of spring beginning to back
up along their veins?
Yonder stand a young boy and girl leaning against a bicycle.
The iron lamppost next to them disappears into the feathery,
unborn leaves that suffocate its top.

A postman is coming up the walk, a letter held in his
outstretched hand.
This is his first day on the new job, and he looks warily around
Alas not seeing the hideous bulldog bearing down on him like sixty,
its hellish eyes fixed on the seat of his pants, jowls a-slaver.

Nearby a young woman is fixing her stocking. Watching her, a
    chap with a hat
Is about to walk into the path of a speeding hackney cabriolet.
    The line of lampposts
Marches up the street in strict array, but the lamp-parts
Are lost in feathery bloom, in which hidden faces can be spotted,
    for this is a puzzle scene.
The sky is white, yet full of outlined stars—it must be night,
Or an early springtime evening, with just a hint of dampness and
    chill in the air—
Memory of winter, hint of the autumn to come—
Yet the lovers congregate anyway, the lights twinkle slowly on.
Cars move steadily along the street.
It is a scene worthy of the poet's pen, yet it is the fire demon
Who has created it, throwing it up on the dubious surface of a
    phosphorescent fountain
For all the world like a poet. But love can appreciate it,
Use or misuse it for its own ends. Love is stronger than fire.

The proof of this is that already the heaving, sucking fountain
    is paling away
Yet the fire-lines of the lovers remain fixed, as if permanently,
    on the air of the lab.
Not for long though. And now they too collapse,
Giving, as they pass away, the impression of a bluff,
Its craggy headlands outlined in sparks, its top crowned with
    a zigzag
Of grass and shrubs, pebbled beach at the bottom, with flat sea
Holding a few horizontal lines. Then this vision, too, fades
    slowly away.

III

Now you must shield with your body if necessary (you
Remind me of some lummox I used to know) the secret your
    body is.
Yes, you are a secret and you must NEVER tell it—the vapor
Of the stars would quickly freeze you to death, like a tear-stiffened
    handkerchief

51

Held in liquid air. No, but this secret is in some way the fuel of
Your living apart. A hearth fire picked up in the glow of polished
Wooden furniture and picture frames, something to turn away
        from and move back to—
Understand? This is all a part of you and the only part of you.

            Here comes the answer: is it because apples grow
            On the tree, or because it is green? One average day
                you may never know
            How much is pushed back into the night, nor what
                may return
            To sulk contentedly, half asleep and half awake
            By the arm of a chair pointed into
            The painting of the hearth fire, or reach, in a coma,
            Out of the garden for foreign students.
            Be sure the giant would know falling asleep, but the
                frozen droplets reveal
            A mixed situation in which the penis
            Scored the offer by fixed marches into what is.
            One black spot remained.

If I should . . . If I said you were there
The . . . towering peace around us might
Hold up the way it breaks—the monsoon
Move a pebble, to the plumbing contract, cataract.
There has got to be only—there is going to be
An accent on the portable bunch of grapes
The time the mildewed sea cast the
Hygrometer too far away. You read into it
The meaning of tears, survey of our civilization.

            Only one thing exists: the fear of death. As widows
                are a prey to loan sharks
            And Cape Hatteras to hurricanoes, so man to the fear
                of dying, to the
            Certainty of falling. And just so it permits him to escape
                from time to time
            Amid fields of boarded-up posters: "Objects, as they
                recede, appear to become smaller

52

And all horizontal receding lines have their vanish-
    ing point upon the line of sight,"
Which is some comfort after all, for our volition to see
    must needs condition these phenomena to a
    certain degree.
But it would be rash to derive too much confidence
    from a situation which, in the last analysis,
    scarcely warrants it.
What I said first goes: sleep, death and hollyhocks
And a new twilight stained, perhaps, a slightly
    unearthlier periwinkle blue,
But no dramatic arguments for survival, and please
    no magic justification of results.

Uh . . . stupid song . . . that weather bonnet
Is all gone now. But the apothecary biscuits dwindled.
Where a little spectral
Cliffs, teeming over into irony's
Gotten silently inflicted on the passages
Morning undermines, the daughter is.

    Its oval armor
    Protects it then, and the poisonous filaments
        hanging down
    Are armor as well, or are they the creature itself,
        screaming
    To protect itself? An aggressive weapon, as well as a
        plan of defense?
    Nature is still liable to pull a few fast ones, which is
        why I can't emphasize enough
    The importance of adhering to my original program.
        Remember,
    No hope is to be authorized except in exceptional cases
    To be decided on by me. In the meantime, back to
        dreaming,
    Your most important activity.

The most difficult of all is an arrangement of hawthorn leaves
But the sawing motion of desire, throwing you a moment

to one side
And then the other, will, I think, permit you to forget your
     dreams for a little while.
In reality you place too much importance on them. "Frei aber
     Einsam" (Free but Alone)
Ought to be your motto. If you dream at all, place a cloth over
     your face:
Its expression of satisfied desire might be too much for some
     spectators.

         The west wind grazes my cheek, the droplets come
              pattering down;
         What matter now whether I wake or sleep?
         The west wind grazes my cheek, the droplets come
              pattering down;
         A vast design shows in the meadow's parched and
              trampled grasses.
         Actually a game of "fox and geese" has been played
              there, but the real reality,
         Beyond truer imaginings, is that it is a mystical design
              full of a certain significance,
         Burning, sealing its way into my consciousness.
         Smooth out the sad flowers, pick up where you left off
         But leave me immersed in dreams of sexual imagery:
         Now that the homecoming geese unfurl in waves on
              the west wind
         And cock covers hen, the farmhouse dog slavers
              over his bitch, and horse and mare go screwing
              through the meadow!
         A pure scream of things arises from these various
              sights and smells
         As steam from a wet shingle, and I am happy once
              again
         Walking among these phenomena that seem familiar
              to me from my earliest childhood.

The gray wastes of water surround
My puny little shoal. Sometimes storms roll
Tremendous billows far up on the gray sand beach, and

54

the morning
After, odd tusked monsters lie stinking in the sun.
They are inedible. For food there is only
Breadfruit, and berries garnered in the jungle's inner reaches,
Wrested from scorpion and poisonous snake. Fresh water is
    a problem.
After a rain you may find some nestling in the hollow trunk
    of a tree, or in hollow stones.

One's only form of distraction is really
To climb to the top of the one tall cliff to scan the distances.
Not for a ship, of course—this island is far from all the
    trade routes—
But in hopes of an unusual sight, such as a school of
    dolphins at play,
A whale spouting, or a cormorant bearing down on its prey.
So high this cliff is that the pebble beach far below seems
    made of gravel.
Halfway down, the crows and choughs look like bees.
Near by are the nests of vultures. They cluck
    sympathetically in my direction,
Which will not prevent them from rending me limb from limb
    once I have keeled over definitively.
Further down, and way over to one side, are eagles;
Always fussing, fouling their big nests, they always seem
    to manage to turn their backs to you.
The glass is low; no doubt we are in for a storm.

Sure enough: in the pale gray and orange distances to the left, a
Waterspout is becoming distinctly visible.
Beautiful, but terrifying;
Delicate, transparent, like a watercolor by that nineteenth-century
    Englishman whose name I forget
(I am beginning to forget everything on this island. If only I had
    been allowed to bring my ten favorite books with me—
But a weathered child's alphabet is my only reading material.
    Luckily,
Some of the birds and animals on the island are pictured in it—
    the albatross, for instance—that's a name I never would

have remembered.)

It looks as though the storm-fiend were planning to kick up
       quite a ruckus
For this evening. I had better be getting back to the tent
To make sure everything is shipshape, weight down
       the canvas with extra stones,
Bank the fire, and prepare myself a little hardtack and tea
For the evening's repast. Still, it is rather beautiful up here,
Watching the oncoming storm. Now the big cloud that was
       in front of the waterspout
Seems to be lurching forward, so that the waterspout, behind it,
       looks more like a three-dimensional photograph.
Above me, the sky is a luminous silver-gray. Yet rain, like
       silver porcupine quills, has begun to be thrown down.
All the lightning is still contained in the big black cloud
       however. Now thunder claps belch forth from it,
Causing the startled vultures to fly forth from their nests.
I really had better be getting back down, I suppose.

Still it is rather fun to linger on in the wet,
Letting your clothes get soaked. What difference does it make?
       No one will scold me for it,
Or look askance. Supposing I catch cold? It hardly matters,
       there are no nurses or infirmaries here
To make an ass of one. A really serious case of pneumonia
       would suit me fine.
Ker-choo! There, now I'm being punished for saying so. Aw,
       what's the use.
I really am starting down now. Good-bye, Storm-fiend.
       Good-bye, vultures.

In reality of course the middle-class apartment I live in is nothing
       like a desert island.
Cozy and warm it is, with a good library and record collection.
Yet I feel cut off from the life in the streets.
Automobiles and trucks plow by, spattering me with filthy slush.
The man in the street turns his face away. Another island-dweller,
       no doubt.

56

In a store or crowded café, you get a momentary impression
        of warmth :
Steam pours out of the espresso machine, fogging the panes
        with their modern lettering
Of a kind that has only been available for about a year. The head-
        lines offer you
News that is so new you can't realize it yet. A revolution
        in Argentina ! Think of it ! Bullets flying through
        the air, men on the move ;
Great passions inciting to massive expenditures of energy,
        changing the lives of many individuals.
Yet it is all offered as "today's news," as if we somehow
        had a right to it, as though it were a part of our lives
That we'd be silly to refuse. Here, have another—crime or
        revolution? Take your pick.

None of this makes any difference to professional exiles like me,
        and that includes everybody in the place.
We go on sipping our coffee, thinking dark or transparent
        thoughts . . .
Excuse me, may I have the sugar. Why certainly—pardon me for
        not having passed it to you.
A lot of bunk, none of them really care whether you
        get any sugar or not.
Just try asking for something more complicated and see
        how far it gets you.
Not that I care anyway, being an exile. Nope, the motley spectacle
        offers no charms whatsoever for me—
And yet—and yet I feel myself caught up in its coils—
Its defectuous movement is that of my reasoning powers—
The main point has already changed, but the masses continue
        to tread the water
Of backward opinion, living out their mandate as though nothing
        had happened.
We step out into the street, not realizing that the street is different,
And so it shall be all our lives ; only, from this moment on, nothing
        will ever be the same again. Fortunately our small pleasures
        and the monotony of daily existence
Are safe. You will wear the same clothes, and your friends will

still want to see you for the same reasons—you fill a definite
place in their lives, and they would be sorry to see you go.

There has, however, been this change, so complete as to
      be invisible:
You might call it . . . "passion" might be a good word.
I think we will call it that for easy reference. This room, now,
      for instance, is all black and white instead of blue.
A few snowflakes are floating in the airshaft. Across the way
The sun was sinking, casting gray
Shadows on the front of the buildings.

Lower your left shoulder.
Stand still and do not seesaw with your body.

Any more golfing hints, Charlie?

Plant your feet squarely. Grasp your club lightly but firmly in the
      hollow of your fingers.
Slowly swing well back and complete your stroke well through,
      pushing to the very end.

"All up and down de whole creation," like magic-lantern slides
      projected on the wall of a cavern: castles, enchanted
      gardens, etc.

The usual anagrams of moonlight—a story
That subsides quietly into plain historical fact.
You have chosen the customary images of youth, old age and death
To keep harping on this traditional imagery. The reader

Will not have been taken in.
He will have managed to find out all about it, the way people do.
The moonlight congress backs out then. And with a cry
He throws the whole business into the flames: books, notes, pencil
      diagrams, everything.

No, the only thing that interests him is day

And its problems. **Freiheit!** **Freiheit!** To be out of these
　　　dusty cells once and for all
Has been the dream of mankind since the beginning of the universe.

His day is breaking over the eastern mountains, at least that's
　　　the way he tells it.
Only the crater of becoming—a sealed consciousness—resists the
　　　profaning mass of the sun.
You who automatically sneer at everything that comes along,
　　　except your own work, of course,
Now feel the curious force of the invasion; its soldiers, all and some,
A part of you the minute they appear. It is as though workmen in
　　　blue overalls
Were constantly bringing on new props and taking others away:
　　　that is how you feel the drama going past you, powerless to
　　　act in it.
To have it all be over! To wake suddenly on a hillside
With a valley far below—the clouds—

That is the penance you have already done:
January, March, February. You are living toward a definition
Of the peaceful appetite, then you see
Them standing around limp and hungry like adjacent clouds.

Soon there is to be exchange of ideas and
Far more beautiful handshake, under the coat of
Weather is undecided right now.
Postpone the explanation.
The election is to be held tomorrow, under the trees.

You felt the months keep coming up
And it is December again,
The snow outside. Or is it June full of sun
And the prudent benefits of sun, but still the postman comes.
The true meaning of some of his letters is slight—

Another time I thought I could see myself.
This too proved illusion, but I could deal with the way
I keep returning on myself like a plank

59

Like a small boat blown away from the wind.

It all ends in a smile somewhere,
Notes to be taken on all this,
And you can see in the dark, of which the night
Is the continuation of your ecstasy and apprehension.

IV

The wind thrashes the maple seed-pods,
The whole brilliant mass comes spattering down.

This is my fourteenth year as governor of C province.
I was little more than a lad when I first came here.
Now I am old but scarcely any wiser.
So little are white hair and a wrinkled forehead a sign of wisdom!

To slowly raise oneself
Hand over hand, lifting one's entire weight;
To forget there was a possibility
Of some more politic movement. That freedom, courage
And pleasant company could exist.
That has always been behind you.

An earlier litigation: wind hard in the tops
Of the baggy eucalyptus branches.

Today I wrote, "The spring is late this year.
In the early mornings there is hoarfrost on the water meadows.
And on the highway the frozen ruts are papered over with ice."

The day was gloves.

How far from the usual statement
About time, ice—the weather itself had gone.

I mean this. Through the years
You have approached an inventory
And it is now that tomorrow

Is going to be the climax of your casual
Statement about yourself, begun
So long ago in humility and false quietude.

The sands are frantic
In the hourglass. But there is time
To change, to utterly destroy
That too-familiar image
Lurking in the glass
Each morning, at the edge of the mirror.

The train is still sitting in the station.
You only dreamed it was in motion.

There are a few travelers on Z high road.
Behind a shutter, two black eyes are watching them.
They belong to the wife of P, the high-school principal.

The screen door bangs in the wind, one of the hinges is loose.
And together we look back at the house.
It could use a coat of paint
Except that I am too poor to hire a workman.
I have all I can do to keep body and soul together
And soon, even that relatively simple task may prove to be beyond
        my powers.

That was a good joke you played on the other guests.
A joke of silence.

One seizes these moments as they come along, afraid
To believe too much in the happiness that might result
Or confide too much of one's love and fear, even in
Oneself.

The spring, though mild, is incredibly wet.
I have spent the afternoon blowing soap bubbles
And it is with a feeling of delight I realize I am
All alone in the skittish darkness.
The birch-pods come clattering down on the weed-grown

marble pavement.
And a curl of smoke stands above the triangular wooden roof.

Seventeen years in the capital of Foo-Yung province!
Surely woman was born for something
Besides continual fornication, retarded only by menstrual cramps.

I had thought of announcing my engagement to you
On the day of the first full moon of X month.

The wind has stopped, but the magnolia blossoms still
Fall with a plop onto the dry, spongy earth.
The evening air is pestiferous with midges.

There is only one way of completing the puzzle:
By finding a hog-shaped piece that is light green shading to
        buff at one side.

It is the beginning of March, a few
Russet and yellow wallflowers are blooming in the border
Protected by moss-grown, fragmentary masonry.

One morning you appear at breakfast
Dressed, as for a journey, in your worst suit of clothes.
And over a pot of coffee, or, more accurately, rusted water
Announce your intention of leaving me alone in this
        cistern-like house.
In your own best interests I shall decide not to believe you.

I think there is a funny sand bar
Beyond the old boardwalk
Your intrigue makes you understand.

"At thirty-two I came up to take my examination
        at the university.
The U wax factory, it seemed, wanted a new general manager.
I was the sole applicant for the job, but it was refused me.
So I have preferred to finish my life
In the quietude of this floral retreat."

62

The tiresome old man is telling us his life story.

Trout are circling under water—

Masters of eloquence
Glisten on the pages of your book
Like mountains veiled by water or the sky.

The "second position"
Comes in the seventeenth year
Watching the meaningless gyrations of flies above a sill.

Heads in hands, waterfall of simplicity.
The delta of living into everything.

The pump is busted. I shall have to get it fixed.

Your knotted hair
Around your shoulders
A shawl the color of the spectrum

Like that marvelous thing you haven't learned yet.

To refuse the square hive,
                              postpone the highest . . .

The apples are all getting tinted
In the cool light of autumn.

The constellations are rising
In perfect order: Taurus, Leo, Gemini.

John Ashbery was born in Rochester in 1927, grew up on a farm in western New York State, and received his education at Deerfield Academy, Harvard University, and Columbia University. From 1955 to 1965 he lived and worked in France, during which time three books of his poems were published in the United States. From 1965 to 1972 he was Executive Editor of *Art News*. He is now Distinguished Professor at the City University of New York's Brooklyn College campus, where he teaches creative writing.

Mr. Ashbery's 1975 volume, *Self-Portrait in a Convex Mirror*, won the Pulitzer Prize, the National Book Award, and the National Book Critics Circle Award. He is a member of the American Academy and Institute of Arts and Letters and the National Academy of Arts and Sciences. Twice named a Guggenheim Fellow, he was awarded the annual fellowship of the Academy of American Poets in 1982 and received Yale University's Bollingen Prize in 1984. In 1985 he received a MacArthur Prize Fellowship and the Lenore Marshall/Nation Poetry Prize. He lives in New York City.